IT'S ALL
IN THE WORDS

A collection of poems, thoughts, and words
from an early-childhood educator, mom,
grandmother, friend, and thinker

Shirley Hoffman

little pink press

Published by Little Pink Press, Beacon, NY 12508

ISBN: 979-8-9906436-3-5

Dedication

This collection of words is dedicated to my mother.
Her struggles were many, and her words were few.
As a young adult, I began to understand her more,
especially when we discovered that she had found a
way to express herself through poetry.

Sometimes it really is "All in the Words."

A special thank you to my grandchildren, Christopher,
Mathew, Wilton, Maddie, Kathryn, Lincoln, Jack,
Avery, and Atticus for providing the artwork
accompanying some of the poems.

After the Rain

After the rain, there are puddles to meet

So out the door go three tiny pairs of feet

to warm squishy mud beneath.

One puddle, two, then three, then four

Each one different than the one before.

A bug, a worm, a sliver of oil that fanned from side to side,

A tiny stone and

a feather from a bird that was flying by.

Tired muddy little feet quietly walking home.

"Don't be sad," I say to them

I hear the raindrops starting again.

A Letter to My New Teacher Self

It's OK...

It's OK to have a plan and then not be able to follow it every single minute of every day.

It's OK to change your room around when it just doesn't work for you or the kids.

It's OK to cry...be angry, sad, upset, all of those feelings have a purpose. Trust me.

It's OK if someone doesn't like you whether it be a parent, a child, or a coworker. It's not you.

Remember...

Kindness is a quality that will carry you through the ups and downs of life.

Use challenges as learning opportunities.

Every single child and family I worked with has taught me something about myself, about being a teacher, and becoming who I am today.

If you are feeling drained after a child disrupts EVERYTHING, imagine how that child is feeling.

Your environment is your platform for everything else. You need to be at peace with your environment, and it will bring peace to you and others.

Listen and watch the children, and they will tell you if the environment is working for them.

It takes time to develop just the right mix of materials; a schedule, and a routine...and then it changes.

You will not remember every child you worked with, but you will remember those few, they are the ones...they are the ones you will remember.

Ask questions, ask lots of questions.

Lean on those around you.

Ask for help.

You have your "work" self and your "you" self. Give each of them what they deserve.

You may feel like you have not helped a child but just being in that space at that time and being present, you have made a difference.

always remember...

If you want to change something, start with yourself.

A special note to myself....

Thank you for taking on challenges, thank you for being a teacher of the young children who walked through your doors

Thank you for never giving up hope.

Preschool Teachers Love to Read Books

Oh, how I love reading to children in my care.

Getting ready, holding steady, all from my teacher chair.

It is an art you know,

Holding the words just so

Knowing when to turn the page and when to linger there

Using the right softness or loudness,

pausing for contemplation, starting conversation.

Classics are the absolute best

Like Carle's caterpillar coming to be, or Sendak's Max hanging from trees

Or when Corduroy loses his button but finds his best friend.

And Pooh! With all of his feelings and all of his words

Just hanging out listening and really being heard

It's quite a lovely thing to see

The love of books at ages four and three.

Your Birth Day

Your birth day is more than just a day for me

It's a sparkle in the nighttime sky

A rainy day to enjoy.

It's a sip of tea,

And a flowing summer breeze.

It's the sound of laughter

And heartfelt tears,

It's the life that you give me year after year.

The Boy in the Middle

Born after the first and before the last

It's funny how time goes by way too fast

So, I send him messages when it's been a while

And this is how it goes

"How are you?"

"Fine."

"What's new?"

"Nothing."

"How are the kids?"

"Good."

"OK, I guess we are good for another few weeks.
Talk to you soon."

"OK."

And we both know for sure what has really been said

is a thousand words of love.

Acorns

How does it happen to be?

that acorns fall from the trees?

Do they get heavy with weight?

or fall from a squirrel's menacing shake.

Either way, they lay on my lawn

And crunch under my feet

and I have to wear shoes

Which I don't like to do.

7

Playing in the Rain

Rainy day

The kids looking out the window

Looking for the sun?

Breakfast done

Circle time fun

What's the weather? What's the weather? What's the weather out today?

Is it sunny? Is it cloudy? Is it raining? Is it snowing? Is it blowing? What's the weather out today?

The weather person reports in his tiny reporter voice

"It's raining. And we can't go outside."

My teacher eyes survey their feelings while scanning the cubbies and propose:

"But what if we did go outside in the rain?"

"Wet"

"Slippery"

"Water"

"We need umbrellas. We don't have umbrellas."

"But…do we really need umbrellas?" I ask.

"We have hoods."

"I have boots!"

"Me too. Mine are red."

Excitement rises

"Let's do it!" I say

Eyes wide. Open mouths turn into smiles

　　Slapppp on the boots

　　　　Zzzzzip up the coats

　　　　　And off we go

　　　　　　Playing in the rain

Summer Tea

Summer time

Come outside

It's soft and cool under the tree

We'll have a sip of summer tea.

I call this Ayden's tree

His placenta lies below

I think it surely helped it grow.

One strong trunk with branches reaching high,
holding every sprout that reached up to the sky.

And although yes, he was the first

Seven more followed him to earth

It is for sure his sibling tree

So come on out, and we'll sip some summer tea.

Full of Verse

I just might be late for work.

I woke up this morning full of verse

(Like my brain was working the night shift.)

so before I take on the tasks of the day,

I have to write down what it tells me to say.

Music and Movement

Dancing, scarves, sticks, and drums

Stirring up some music fun

Tapping toes, jumping beans

Circle round and round

Listen to, singing too,

Tired laughing little ones

"Is music time really done?"

Trauma

The new word was "trauma-informed care"

And it was powerful, to give them a place to heal.

But what was more powerful

Was that we were already doing it.

The Paint Job

By Jimmie Ruth Worley (my Mom)

I slept in a room where the paint on the wall was
an ugly color of green.

In fact it was the ugliest green

Of any green that you have ever seen.

I sat down and thought for a while

And decided to paint it myself

So I purchased a beautiful color of gold

and took the brushes down from the shelf.

I painted all day and half of the night

And when I was finished is was really a sight.

The floor was spotted and so was I

When I looked at the walls I started to cry.

I hung up the drapes and pulled down the shades

It was such an ugly sight that when it was dark, I didn't turn on the lights.

About six months later my sister decided to come and stay for a while

She went into the room and turned on the light

The very first look gave her a fright.

She got out the paint and started to work

What she did was a fine sight to see

Well all I could say when I saw the results was,

"God gave her a talent he didn't give me."

She had to travel some six hundred miles to get to where I live

I really enjoyed her visit

The only thing is, I have six more rooms to go

Sure hope she comes again soon.

The Vanity

A tribute to my mom

Like my mother before me
I cannot paint. Not a single stroke looks like it should.
I feel so sorry for the beautiful wood.

My talent is better with painting words
Or telling stories and poems that should be heard.

She painted a room once, my mother she did, trying to save it
from the ugliest color green that you ever have seen
(As told in a poem about that painted day, and her sister while
visiting quickly opened the lid,
and fixed it right up,,,, painted it right with a bit of a fuss
All in good fun of course said my mother's rhyming words.

So,
My mom had a vanity which I did acquire
And one day my daughter said it was her desire…
To paint it.
She began as I watched her work
And I knew her talent was far better than ours
she had it stripped and ready in just a few hours.

But when she opened the doors to begin in there I jumped up
and said, "Look at that ugly color of green with gold spots all
over the place!"

Unmistakably it was the work of my mother.
My aunt must have missed this furniture's doom
or was just too exhausted from fixing the ugly painted room.

We ran out of time as her visit was over.
The project sitting undone,
sat calling my name, "Try again, try again."

I tried. Oh how I tried
I was sure I'd get it right.
And I said that I would while my husband sat tight
He gave me approving nods and a distant face
Seeing the paint all over the place.

But like my mother before me
It's just not meant to be
So I left the inside that ugly gold spotted color green.

Maybe a grandchild will come to be
That will look upon my vanity and think
quietly to no one "that's just like me."

Our painting skills are what they are … my mother and me.
And our vanity will carry every last stroke
A memory to hold a tradition of old.

For whoever takes this piece of art will also take a piece of
my heart.

Granny

I remember...

Her long white hair tied with a simple piece of kitchen string

Seemed like she never left the kitchen.

Stoking the old wood cook stove which she used every day,
even though she had an electric oven in the "new kitchen."

Biscuits and gravy and farm fresh eggs

Her big round wooden bowl for biscuit making kept in a
cupboard that had a bin that pulled forward

It was always full of soft white flour.

The bowl would be readied, sifted flour waiting, balanced on
the cupboard countertop.

She always knew just the right amount of flour for the
morning's biscuits, whether it be 5 or 15

Her measurements came from her soul, not from a measuring cup.

A bit of buttermilk in the center, and she would start swirling until
the dough was right ready for rolling and dropping into the cast iron
skillet that she would heave over to the cook stove.

Shuffling along, one leg shorter than the other

She wore one platform shoe to make up the difference.

The biscuits cooking inside the perfectly hot stove

Eggs frying on top with the bacon next to that.

I learned there's a certain smell of biscuits when you know they are done.

No timer needed in that old kitchen of hers.

Biscuits out, gravy stirring.

On some days it was Grandad in front of the stove

Come back from milking the cows.

Gravy was his perfection,

Nothing else he ever cooked.

I must have followed her step by step every morning I was there

Just to see this magic happen

And to eat those biscuits.

Only I Alone

When I carried you in my womb, I shared you with no one

Every flutter, hiccup, and heartbeat were mine and mine alone.

I fell in love with you, and I couldn't let you go.

Only I alone will remember the flutters, the movements, the stirs in the night,

Your heartbeat so connected to mine,

just so you know, I can never really let you go.

When you were born, your dad had to hold you and just look at you,

He fell in love with you, and I had to let you go.

When I brought you home that day, our families wanted to be a part of your life.

They fell in love with you, and I had to let you go.

When you grew up all too fast, you fell in love

so I had to let you go.

Now another day comes.

You are beginning a new part of your life

And I have to let you go.

But only I alone remember the flutters, the stirs in the night,

Your heartbeat so connected to mine.

And just so you know, I can never really let you go.

The Swing

Sitting on the porch, a grandchild on each side

Under a cozy blanket, watching the stars in the night sky

Another came out to say,

"Let's go in the yard and play!"

Me, feeling a little sad, "I'm feeling pretty comfy here."

The snuggler to the right sighs and says,

"Yeah, this is perfect."

That's love.

Upside Down

It's 8:30 on a mid-September evening

The red, pink fluffy clouds are ushering in the night

It won't be but a few more minutes before someone somewhere has a mirror image of my sky

My thoughts will be theirs only upside down.

Hannah

"Food, I can taste it again." she said.

"And coffee, how wonderful."

Her eyes caught mine

and in them I saw the years of pain

And the hope for tomorrow.

I saw the reflection of her blonde-haired children

So dear to her heart, her reason for living and for
leaving, her strength.

She couldn't sit still

Her mind wouldn't let her

So trained to fear, protect, and hide

But still in those brief few minutes when she did
connect,

the power she held within, deep as it was, shone
through those eyes of blue

"I will be ok; I have friends now."

They Knew

They knew

They didn't understand

But they knew

He was gone

Not coming back

I don't even remember the words I used to tell them

How do you explain to preschoolers that their friend died in a car crash?

Searching for the right words

We drew pictures of him and made a book and the words came from the kids

"The Boy with the Orange-Colored Hair"

Being Remembered

It was a Friday night

After a long week.

New staff

Starting up a new classroom,

doing five jobs to keep things going,

and I got a message on my phone.

"We are sitting by the fire, and your name came up so I wanted to say hi. How is your family? How are you?"

I felt so humbled.

I filled her in on things and said how are the kids?

"Jason is in 7th grade. Josey likes baseball, and June is doing well.

She gets speech services, and it really helps."

She sent me a picture.

From a preschooler to a 7th grader, and they still care enough to not only think of me but to reach out and give me a the gift of remembrance.

It is then that I realize my tired Friday night is worth it.

Grey Becomes Me

It started with a little spot.

There it was on the back of my head right on top

Lay tiny wisps of grey.

And I fought it with the colors of my youth

Brown with tints of red.

It became a battle all and out

But the grey was winning without a doubt.

And then it all made sense to me

My grey saying, "Hey, it's OK."

"You'll love the change that will come to be."

I Wonder

I have almost lost their attention.

Now is the time.

I hold something in my closed-fisted hand

and say, "I wonder what this is?"

Attention is back...all eyes on me.

I open my hand very slowly

And we go mind exploring

Taking guesses

All are in.

And then, I pass this thing around and ask once more

"Tell me something that you didn't before."

Like magic, more words start to fill the air

"It's squishy, it's red, it's soft, it's like a ball."

And they start thinking, really thinking

The thinking is so very good

But this time, THIS time I've got them!

Next, I show them how to use this thing, and they are all surprised.

We use it the rest of the day and the words keep filling the air.

The Memories I Hold

Coffeetea said the little one,
Pailnolish said the other.

And Did you hear that pokerpack? said their brother.

The memories I hold the words I hear.

Watching the sun setting over the trees
And he thought it went there because of me,

Rainy days and mud puddle jumps,

The sparkles in the dark night sky.

The memories I hold the words I hear.

Stopping the wind so she wouldn't be scared and lose hope
In that storm in a tent that we held down with a rope

The sleepless nights because of nightmares from the past
And leg aches that needed to be healed fast

The memories I hold, the words I hear

And in just a few days I'll be one year older it's true
Thank goodness my life is still blessed with you and you and you.

The memories I hold the words I hear.

Illustrations

After The Rain: Wilton
Preschool Teachers Love To Read Books: Atticus
Acorns: Avery
Full Of Verse: Maddie
Granny: Kathryn
The Swing: Matthew
They Knew: Lincoln
Being Remembered: Jack
The Memories I Hold: Christopher